"It's our insides that make us who we are, that allow us to dream and wonder and feel for others. That's what's essential. That's what will always make the biggest difference in our world."

—Fred Rogers

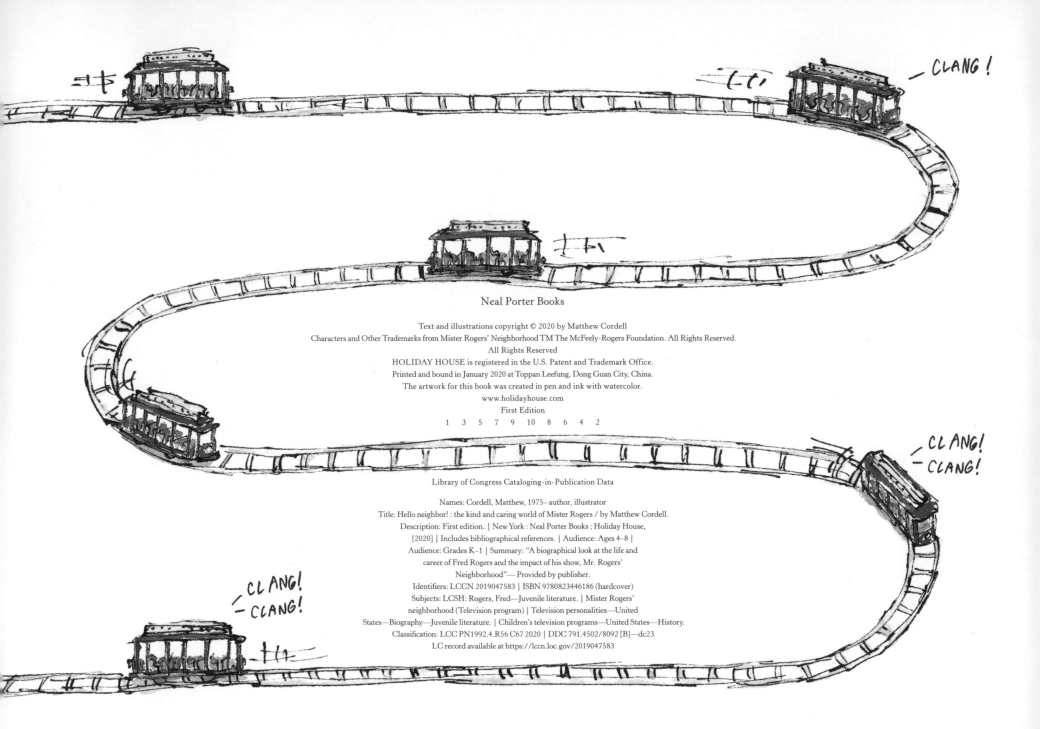

Neal Porter Books

Text and illustrations copyright © 2020 by Matthew Cordell
Characters and Other Trademarks from Mister Rogers' Neighborhood TM The McFeely-Rogers Foundation. All Rights Reserved.
All Rights Reserved
HOLIDAY HOUSE is registered in the U.S. Patent and Trademark Office.
Printed and bound in January 2020 at Toppan Leefung, Dong Guan City, China.
The artwork for this book was created in pen and ink with watercolor.
www.holidayhouse.com
First Edition
1   3   5   7   9   10   8   6   4   2

Library of Congress Cataloging-in-Publication Data

Names: Cordell, Matthew, 1975– author, illustrator
Title: Hello neighbor! : the kind and caring world of Mister Rogers / by Matthew Cordell.
Description: First edition. | New York : Neal Porter Books ; Holiday House,
[2020] | Includes bibliographical references. | Audience: Ages 4–8 |
Audience: Grades K–1 | Summary: "A biographical look at the life and
career of Fred Rogers and the impact of his show, Mr. Rogers'
Neighborhood"— Provided by publisher.
Identifiers: LCCN 2019047583 | ISBN 9780823446186 (hardcover)
Subjects: LCSH: Rogers, Fred—Juvenile literature. | Mister Rogers'
neighborhood (Television program) | Television personalities—United
States—Biography—Juvenile literature. | Children's television programs—United States—History.
Classification: LCC PN1992.4.R56 C67 2020 | DDC 791.4502/8092 [B]—dc23
LC record available at https://lccn.loc.gov/2019047583

HELLO, NEIGHBOR!

The Kind and Caring World of Mister Rogers

Matthew Cordell

NEAL PORTER BOOKS
HOLIDAY HOUSE / NEW YORK

Welcome to Mister Rogers' Neighborhood.

As you can see, this is no ordinary neighborhood.

It's the set for a television program. A children's television program that's connected with countless families since it was first broadcast nationally in 1968.

There were many things that made it different from your neighborhood. There were actors, camera operators, musicians, stage sets, and puppets. It took a great deal of work and love to bring The Neighborhood to life each day.

And it was all started by a man named Fred McFeely Rogers.

Growing up near Pittsburgh, Pennsylvania, Fred had many interests.

He especially loved playing with puppets and music.

He learned to play the piano at the age of five.

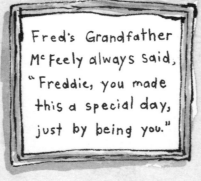

Fred playing his first piano.

Fred's Grandfather McFeely always said, "Freddie, you made this a special day, just by being you."

Fred playing with his baby sister, Elaine.

Fred's family was proud of his talent and encouraged him to study music and composition as he got older.

Fred playing the piano Grandmother McFeely bought him when he was nine years old.

Fred was shy and often lonely. He was sometimes bullied. But whimsy
and imagination were helpful to him and so was his faith. After college,
he planned to become a minister, and years later he did become a
special kind of minister. But at this moment in his life, something
unexpected happened.

In those days, television was new and just beginning to become popular. And Fred didn't like what
he saw. "I saw people throwing pies in each others' faces, and all kinds of demeaning behavior . . . and
I thought, 'Why is it being used in this way? This could be a wonderful tool for education.' And so I
said to my parents, 'You know . . . I think maybe I'll go into television.'" So he went to work for the
National Broadcasting Company (NBC) in New York City to learn how television programs are made.

At first, Fred simply ran errands and fetched things
that were needed around the studio.
And he learned a great deal.

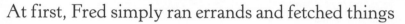

Best of all, he learned that connecting
with younger viewers through children's
television was what he loved the most.

Fred moved back to Pittsburgh and began working on a television program for children. He continued to stay behind the scenes, but he took on a more creative role. Drawing on his background in music, he wrote songs and created characters, returning to his childhood love of puppetry.

As an adult, Fred remembered the wonder of childhood as well as the fears. He spent a lot of time studying and learning about children and about their needs and feelings. And in time, it became obvious to him that too much of children's television was no more than silly and flashy entertainment.

Fred had a new mission: to create a very different kind of children's television program that spoke to its audience with respect and understanding. A program where Fred would perform, as never before, in front of the camera and speak directly to his audience. And he would simply be his honest self. Curious and playful. Attentive and compassionate.

On February 19, 1968, Fred became a permanent resident of *Mister Rogers'*
Neighborhood, when it premiered nationally on public television.

And now . . .

Welcome back to The Neighborhood! Fred began every episode by singing his welcoming song and changing into his comfortable cardigan sweater and sneakers.

Let's make the most of this beautiful day...

Since we're together we might as well say...

Would you be mine, could you be mine, Won't you be my neighbor?

Then a new idea, person, or place would be introduced. Just like in life, there were good times in The Neighborhood, like visiting the circus or a neighborhood school.

But there were difficult times too, like saying goodbye to a beloved pet. Fred understood that children have many feelings and interests, and all of them are worth mentioning and exploring.

Mister Rogers had many regular visitors, like Mr. McFeely, a friend who brought deliveries and discoveries. And Joe Negri, who owned a nearby music store.

MR. M^cFEELY
Speedy Delivery

BETTY ABERLIN
Betty's Little Theater

FRANÇOIS CLEMMONS
Police Officer

AUDREY ROTH
Audrey's Cleaning Service

CHEF BROCKETT
Brockett's Bakery

MAGGIE STEWART
Neighborhood friend

CHUCK ABER
Neighborhood friend

JOE NEGRI
Negri's Music Shop

BOB TROW
Trow's Workshop

ELSIE NEAL
Neighborhood Craft Shop

Welcoming and accepting others and their differences was of great importance in The Neighborhood. Fred made sure to include a diverse range of actors performing important roles. Police Officer Clemmons was the first African American character to appear in a recurring role on a children's television series.

Fred realized that children were naturally curious about the world around them. So, as Mister Rogers, he often took us out of his home to meet new people and discover new places. We found out how people make things, and how workers do their jobs.

ERIC CARLE

We even met world-famous artists in The Neighborhood, like Eric Carle, Yo-Yo Ma, and Margaret Hamilton.

YO-YO MA

Each day in The Neighborhood, we spent time pretending when Trolley took us from Fred's television house to The Neighborhood of Make-Believe.

MARGARET HAMILTON

CLANG! CLANG!

TO MAKE-BELIEVE

Here in The Neighborhood of Make-Believe, an ensemble cast of puppets and people acted out a story about the subject introduced in the beginning of each episode.

Henrietta
Pussycat

X
the Owl

Lady Elaine
Fairchilde

Ana
Platypus

Daniel
Striped Tiger

Mayor
Maggie

Purple
Panda

Elsie Jean
Platypus

Dr. Bill
Platypus

Lady
Aberlin

When Mister Rogers visited a school, The Neighborhood of Make-Believe built a school. When we saw how people make crayons in his real neighborhood, The Neighborhood of Make-Believe held a coloring contest.

Fred loved the expressive and connective nature of playing and listening to music. So lots of music was played throughout The Neighborhood. A jazz trio played the background music throughout the program. And, of course, each day in The Neighborhood, Fred sang the songs he had composed.

JOHNNY COSTA TRIO
Johnny Costa, Bobby Rawsthorne, and Carl McVicker Jr.

Throughout his career, Fred wrote hundreds of songs about the important
things children feel and learn as they grow, like "Many Ways to Say I Love You,"
"What Do You Do with the Mad that You Feel?," and "It's You I Like."

It's you I like... every part of you... your skin, your eyes,
your feelings... whether old or new...

...It's you I like.

Every visit to The Neighborhood would end as it began. Mister Rogers changed back into his jacket and dress shoes while singing his song of love and reassurance, to let us know he would be back next time.

It's such a good feeling to know you're alive!

It's such a happy feeling you're growing inside!...

It's such a good feeling... a very good feeling... the feeling you know that we're friends.

Fred played many roles in the making of more than 900 episodes of *Mister Rogers'*
Neighborhood. He wrote the scripts. He was songwriter and singer, performer and
puppeteer. He oversaw and approved what went on in every episode. Beyond his own
contributions, he truly loved working with others. He respected and appreciated the
talents and artistry of all who were involved in the creation of *Mister Rogers' Neighborhood*.
And because of this, everyone felt connected in a very sincere and personal way.

Just like a real neighborhood.

Just like yours.

About Fred Rogers

FRED ROGERS was born in the small town of Latrobe, Pennsylvania, on March 20, 1928. He was the child of a very loving and spiritual family, and one that had great success in the business of brick manufacturing. So, it was somewhat expected that Fred would do the same when he finished college. But his interests in childhood development and music led him to a life in children's television instead.

His career in TV began when he moved to New York City after college to work for NBC as a floor manager for a number of programs. It was in this time that Fred was married to his college sweetheart, Joanne, a fellow musician. The couple moved back to Pittsburgh in 1953, where Fred worked as a program manager for public television station WQED. Soon after, Fred helped to start the children's television program *The Children's Corner*. The primary performer on the show was Josie Carey, and Fred stayed behind the scenes working as co-producer, puppeteer, organist, and composer. *The Children's Corner* was loved for its lively and lighthearted spirit, and it ran a successful eight years.

In the years that followed *The Children's Corner*, Fred continued working in television. His format was evolving, as was his family. Fred continued his education, taking graduate courses in child development and studying at Pittsburgh Theological Seminary. He was ordained a Presbyterian minister with a special charge of serving children and families through television. He and Joanne had two children, James and John. In 1962, Fred moved with his family to Canada to produce a fifteen-minute program called *Misterogers*. He was appearing in front of the camera now, speaking directly to his many young viewers. Fred continued writing songs, now performing them himself. And the tone of his program became more serious and deep, yet maintaining some of the light and playful attitude he was becoming known for.

In 1964, the family moved back to Pittsburgh for good. And in the next few years Fred began developing the program that would solidify his impact in children's television and maintain his focus for the rest of his life. *Mister Rogers' Neighborhood* debuted locally in 1966 and was broadcast nationally for the first time on February 19, 1968.

Fred Rogers with King Friday XIII.

The Neighborhood provided a place of calm, quiet, and strength to children everywhere. As time went on, the simplicity and sincerity of the program was in stark contrast to much of the fast-paced cynicism seen in the world of children's entertainment and in the world at large. But Fred resisted trends and pressure to change his format. He chose public television from the beginning because there was no advertising, and he found a wonderful partner in PBS. He wanted what was best for children, above all else.

Mister Rogers' Neighborhood went on to become one of the most successful and longest-running children's television programs in history with more than 900 episodes completed by the end of its production in 2001. The program continues to be celebrated by children and grown-ups all over.

Fred died on February 27, 2003, at the age of 74. But his legacy lives on. Fred Rogers Productions in Pittsburgh still thrives and is dedicated to infusing his spirit of quality and care into new television programs for children. Their flagship program, *Daniel Tiger's Neighborhood*, is a direct nod to Fred Rogers and the many beloved characters made popular by *Mister Rogers' Neighborhood*. And just as important in continuing his message are the many children who connected with Fred. Those children have grown up now to become parents themselves—parents who still share his timeless and important messages of love, acceptance, kindness, and individuality with their own children and with those to come.

Fred and The Neighborhood cast.

Fred and Trolley.

On The Neighborhood set.

Behind the scenes in The Neighborhood of Make-Believe.

Visiting with children in a Chicago school.

Visual Glossary

 A traffic light flashed yellow at the beginning of each episode of *Mister Rogers' Neighborhood*, providing viewers with a signal to slow down from time to time, to take in the people and things happening around us.

 Josie Carey partnered with Fred on *The Children's Corner* in his earliest days producing children's television. Josie was the host and primary performer, while Fred kept behind the scenes as puppeteer of characters like Daniel Striped Tiger and King Friday XIII.

 143 was a favorite number of Fred's as he translated it to the number of letters of each word in "I love you." He also made a point in weighing exactly 143 lbs. for much of his adult life.

 Daniel Striped Tiger lives in a large grandfather clock. The face of this clock has no hands because in The Neighborhood of Make-Believe, we can pretend it's any time we like.

 Fred Rogers once had an endearing meeting with Koko, the gorilla known and beloved around the world for her gentle spirit and understanding of American Sign Language. Koko, a fan of *Mister Rogers' Neighborhood*, saw Fred and cradled him in her massive arms. She even untied his shoelaces and took his sneakers off, just as she saw him do on television.

 One particular touching moment from *Mister Rogers' Neighborhood* was when Fred welcomed onto the program a boy he had met while traveling. Jeff Erlanger joined Fred for a mostly unscripted segment where he spoke a bit about his disability and together they sang, "It's You I Like."

 When *Mister Rogers' Neighborhood* debuted in 1968, it was broadcast in black and white. The first color episode aired in 1971.

 There was a fish tank in Mister Rogers' television home. On many programs, he would delight in saying hello to the fish and feeding them.

 Once, Fred's car was stolen. Mister Rogers was so beloved that when word got out, the car was promptly returned to its spot, with an anonymous note that read, "If we'd known it was yours, we never would have taken it."

 *Mister Rogers' Neighborhood* opened with the camera overlooking a small model neighborhood. When Fred visited new places in programs, new buildings would be added to the model for continuity.

 Fred was fluent in French and he enjoyed providing the voice of Grandpére (the French word for Grandfather) to expose children to another language.

Mister Rogers and Me

As a child of the late 1970s and early 1980s, I grew up watching *Mister Rogers' Neighborhood*. Even as a preschooler, I think I had a sense that Mister Rogers and his television program were loving, sincere, and creative in ways that were very different from anything else on TV. But as I grew older and into an adult, my interests changed many times over. I thought less and less about Mister Rogers until the year my wife, Julie, and I welcomed a child of our own into the world.

After our daughter, Romy, was born, Julie and I found ourselves tuning into PBS children's programming again. Most of what was on were newer programs, but our local PBS station also ran episodes of *Mister Rogers' Neighborhood*. And when I saw him again, it was a surprisingly emotional reunion.

Some of the feelings I was having were from memories of my childhood and my connection to Mister Rogers. But tuning in day after day, I was struck by how kind, patient, and selfless Mister Rogers seemed. In a world that is too often fast-paced and insincere, it was refreshing to listen to and watch Mister Rogers and the many Neighborhood characters through the ears and eyes of a parent and an adult. And I had forgotten how unique and playful the format of the program was. A central character speaking to television viewers. Daily teaching moments and sparking of curiosity. Unusual characters and puppets and set changes. And so much wonderful music.

I was compelled to dig deeper and to learn more about the man behind the program. Most people who play characters on television are very different in their real lives. But I was surprised to learn that the real Fred Rogers was essentially the same person as the Mister Rogers he played on television. Creative and playful. Focused and driven. Kind and generous. Calm and patient. The more I learned about his work and life, the more inspired I became. I felt there needed to be a picture book that shared the story of Fred Rogers and *Mister Rogers' Neighborhood* with today's child.

I feel immensely blessed and honored to be able to showcase the world of Fred Rogers to families all over in the best way I know how: with the love and respect that I hope shines through with each page of this book.

Acknowledgments

This book is the result of a lot of love, patience, and collaboration, and would never have been possible without the generosity and support of my own neighborhood. Thank you to Neal Porter, Jennifer Browne, and everyone at Holiday House for getting behind this book from the very beginning and for bringing it to life. Thank you to my literary agent, Rosemary Stimola, for always believing in me and for the unrelenting love and support. Thank you to my family, Julie, Romy, and Dean, for your endless inspiration and for making each and every one of my days a special day. Thank you to Emily Uhrin and the Fred Rogers Center for providing me with the time and visual resources I needed to create this book. Special thanks to Fred Rogers Productions, for your trust and faith in me, and for providing the invaluable history, insight, and guidance that made this book and experience as perfect as can be. Thank you especially to Cathy Cohen Droz, Kevin Morrison, David Newell, Hedda Sharapan, Matthew Shiels, Brittany Smith, Micah Southwood, and Margy Whitmer. And, of course, thank you immensely to Fred Rogers for the kindness, truth, and wisdom that inspires me and so many others daily. There was only one person in the world exactly like you. And we will always love you for the many gifts you shared with us all.

More About Fred Rogers

DOCUMENTARY FILM

Won't You Be My Neighbor?, directed by Morgan Neville, Universal Studios Home Entertainment, 2017

WEBSITES

misterrogers.org

fredrogers.org

fredrogerscenter.org

Where to Watch Mister Rogers' Neighborhood

Episodes of *Mister Rogers' Neighborhood* are available for viewing at:

https://www.misterrogers.org/watch/

Amazon Prime Video

Your local PBS affiliate—check local listings.

"You are a very special person. There is only one person like you in the whole world. There has never been anyone exactly like you before, and there will never be again. And people can like you just because you're you."

—Fred Rogers